THE DAY THE SKY FELL IN

The Day the Sky Fell In is a therapeutic story about letting go of worries and emotional baggage. When a determined girl climbs a difficult path up a cliff, the sky rains down mystery objects on her which she catches and carries with her. Her journey becomes more and more difficult and when she arrives at the top of the cliff she is too weighed down to slide down to the sea, the very place she wants to get to. By letting go of things she doesn't really need, the girl feels lighter and is able to follow her valued direction. This beautifully illustrated storybook will appeal to all children, and can be used by practitioners, educators and parents as a tool to discuss with children what we value as important in life and how we can let go of things we don't need, such as unhealthy or unhelpful feelings, thoughts or behaviours.

Juliette Ttofa is a Specialist Senior Educational Psychologist with 15 years' experience working with children and young people. She specialises in supporting resilience and well-being in vulnerable children.

Julia Gallego is a picture book illustrator and designer, and a graduate of the Manchester School of Art.

For Tori Amos
and all the other red-headed mermaids out there

First published 2018 by Routledge
2 Park Square, Milton Park, Abingdon, Oxon OX14 4RN

52 Vanderbilt Avenue, New York, NY 10017

Routledge is an imprint of the Taylor & Francis Group, an informa business

British Library Cataloguing-in-Publication Data
A catalogue record for this book is available from the British Library

Library of Congress Cataloging-in-Publication Data
A catalog record for this book has been requested

ISBN: 978-1-138-30888-6 (pbk)
ISBN: 978-1-315-14319-4 (ebk)

Typeset in Calibri
by Apex CoVantage, LLC

The Day the Sky Fell In

A Story About Finding Your Element

Juliette Ttofa

Illustrated by Julia Gallego

Routledge
Taylor & Francis Group

LONDON AND NEW YORK

There was once a little girl who dreamed of going to the sea-side.

Every morning she would wake thinking of the sea
and then go to bed sad at the thought of never seeing it.

So one day she rode her bike down to the sea with nothing but a knapsack and a rope.

But when she arrived, she found the strange path to the beach was long and difficult.

1

It had steep steps up to a cliff-top

and then a smooth, slippery slope down,
just like a slide.

The steps were as thin as the blade of a
knife and as high as a beanstalk.

And she found them very hard to climb –
but she took it one step at a time.

It was Autumn, and
crimson leaves lifted
in the wind,

scattering like a chatter
of starlings at sunset.

It began to rain.

But then the girl made out something else tumbling from the orange
clouds – the sky seemed to be falling!

3

Frogs and insects, then cats and dogs, showered down and around like hail.

But the girl kept on climbing.

Other objects fell from the sky too. She tried to catch them.

Some might be useful later, she thought, as she climbed up higher...

First, she caught a scarf and gloves,
a bobbly hat, some thick, woolly socks
and a cagoule.

Then, some
binoculars, a
checked blanket,
a flask, and
an all-in-one
snow suit.

The weary little girl
tried to carry the objects but it was difficult.
So she yanked the rope out of her knapsack and tied the objects to it.
It tugged her down.
But she kept on climbing.

Then came Winter...

The rickety steps shook in the icy wind.

The girl's eyes smarted in the frost.

Her hands turned numb with cold so she put on the gloves, scarf and bobbly hat.

But as she stumbled higher and higher up the ladder still more objects fell...

Down came a tennis racket,
a fishing net,
a cricket bat and
a ball.
After that some sticky sun cream,

some smelly insect repellent,
a rubber ring, a book
and a torch.
Her legs felt so heavy,
but she kept on climbing.

Then, the girl reached the top of the steps

and it was almost Spring!

Blackbirds began to sing and make nests in the trees.

But just as the girl thought it was safe, March winds and April rains came and snatched away her hat, scarf and gloves. Her fingers slipped on the metal rungs – but she held on tight for as long as she could.

And she kept climbing.

Some playing cards,
deck-chairs fished out from
a river, a twirling parasol,
an inflatable dinghy,
a stripy beach towel, a bucket
and spade, a swimming costume
and a wicker picnic basket
all came hurtling towards the girl.

Last of all, a beach tent, a windbreak, a folding table and chairs, and even a disposable barbecue.

The little girl's body was pulled down by the weight of all the objects tied onto the rope, like the tail of a kite.

Way up, as high as a mountain, she almost lost her footing.

But she kept climbing.

Then she heard a sound.
It was the sweet sound of seagulls.
A warm sea-breeze gently caressed the girl's face.
And as she climbed one more step she discovered
she had reached the very top.

The little girl sat at the top in relief and bathed in the sunlight.
Then she looked forward towards the sparkling sea;
it glistened like thousands and thousands of tiny diamonds
and was brighter and more beautiful than
anything she had ever seen in her life.
Salty sea-air tousled her wavy,
auburn hair – a rippling
red prayer flag trailing
in the wind.

The little girl's hand held
on, tight as a bud, to the end of
the rope.

She took one last look at the distant Winter, which lay at the bottom of the steps, and
then, she tried to slide down to the sea.

But she sat still - not moving up
or down.

For the objects on the rope were too heavy to be pulled up to the very top
of the steps and her body was too light to drag them down.

It felt like the forces of nature were conspiring against her, and she
let out a little cry.

But, taking a deep breath in, the young girl knew what she had to do.

"Maybe I don't need to keep holding on to everything," she thought. "Maybe I could try letting go of things that don't matter and just keep the things I love."

She put just a few of her favourite things in her knapsack, and, closing her eyes, she let go of the rope.

"Wheeeeeeeeeeeeeeeeeeeeeeeeeeeeeeee!!!!!"

15 She slid all the way down towards the sea.

The rope ricocheted away with all of the things she had been carrying thundering to the bottom of the steps with a giant thud.

Slipping down the slide, the little girl felt so much lighter.

She wondered why she hadn't let go of everything sooner.

The objects had been weighing her down so much and she didn't really need all those things.

16

As her body pierced the surface of the sea and she plunged into the depths, the water fizzed around her.

And then she saw it –

cautiously unfurling like a delicate leaf...

Her tail.

Her beautiful, shimmering, scalloped tail, where her feet had once been.

No wonder she had found it so difficult to climb the ladder, she thought – she was a mermaid and she belonged in the sea!

The little mermaid swirled around in the clear water.

Strong and supple now, sunlight bounced off her scales, refracting through the water in new directions.

She floated like a dream.

The sky had stopped falling, the Summer was here and it felt good.